Civil W

Author
Illustrator   Barb Lorseyedi

Reproducible for classroom use only.
Not for use by an entire school or school system.

EP108 ©Highsmith® Inc. 1996, 2002, 2007
W5527 State Road 106, P.O. Box 800
Fort Atkinson, WI 53538

Table of Contents

The Home Front
Background	3
Slavery	5
Underground Railroad	6
Aid Societies	8
Civil War Homes	9
Men's Clothing	10
Women's Clothing	12
Jewelry and Accessories	14
Photography	16
Bank Notes	18

The War Front
Uniforms	20
Tents and Shelters	21
Soldiers' Supplies	22
Haversacks	24
"Housewife"	25
Medicine	26
Clara Barton	27
Camp Portraits	28
Regimental Flags	30
Buglers and Drummers	31
Music	32
Camp Recreation	34
Newspapers	35
Correspondents	36
Medal of Honor	37
Battlefield Food	38

People
Jefferson Davis	40
Abraham Lincoln	41
Ulysses S. Grant	44
Robert E. Lee	45
General Sherman	46

Resources
Literature List	47
Glossary	48

The Hands-on Heritage series has been designed to help you bring culture to life in your classroom! Look for the "For the Teacher" headings to find information to help you prepare for activities. Simply block out these sections when reproducing pages for student use.

Background

The period of the Civil War was a very bloody and troubling era in United States history. Although slavery was a major issue of the Civil War, it was not the only concern that was dividing the Union in the late 1800s. There was much economic rivalry between the Northern and Southern states. Since the North was developing an industrial economy, it favored high tariffs (taxes) on imports from Europe to protect its own manufactured goods. The South, whose economy was primarily agricultural, preferred low tariffs so it could import cheap goods from Europe.

Another issue was states' rights versus a strong central government. Southern states wanted the right to nullify (override) federal laws that they did not agree with or particularly like. Representatives in Congress also disagreed over where the proposed transcontinental railroad lines should be built. Northerners wanted the railroad to follow a northern route; Southerners wanted a route that would benefit the South.

All these issues played a part in separating the Northern states from the Southern states. Everything came to a head when South Carolina was the first state to secede from the Union on December 20, 1860. Within six weeks, Texas, Florida, Mississippi, Georgia, Louisiana, and Alabama joined in the secession. By March of 1861, these states had met in Montgomery, Alabama, and formed the Confederate States of America, naming Jefferson Davis as the president of their Confederacy.

Aside from the war itself, we will examine other aspects of life and society during this troubling period.

Project
Learn about the geographic split in the United States during the Civil War by completing the map activity.

Materials
- Civil War Map
- two different-colored markers or crayons

Directions
1. Identify the states and the Mississippi River on the map.
2. Using the information above, color all the states that seceded from the union in one color.
3. Then color all the Union states in the second color.
4. Answer the two questions on the map page.

For the Teacher
Copy one Civil War Map (page 4) per student.

Confederate States
Alabama	Louisiana	Tennessee
Arkansas	Mississippi	Texas
Florida	North Carolina	Virginia
Georgia	South Carolina	

Union States
Connecticut	Maryland	Ohio
Delaware	Massachusetts	Pennsylvania
Illinois	Michigan	Rhode Island
Indiana	Minnesota	Vermont
Iowa	Missouri	West Virginia
Kansas	New Hampshire	Wisconsin
Kentucky	New Jersey	
Maine	New York	

Civil War Map

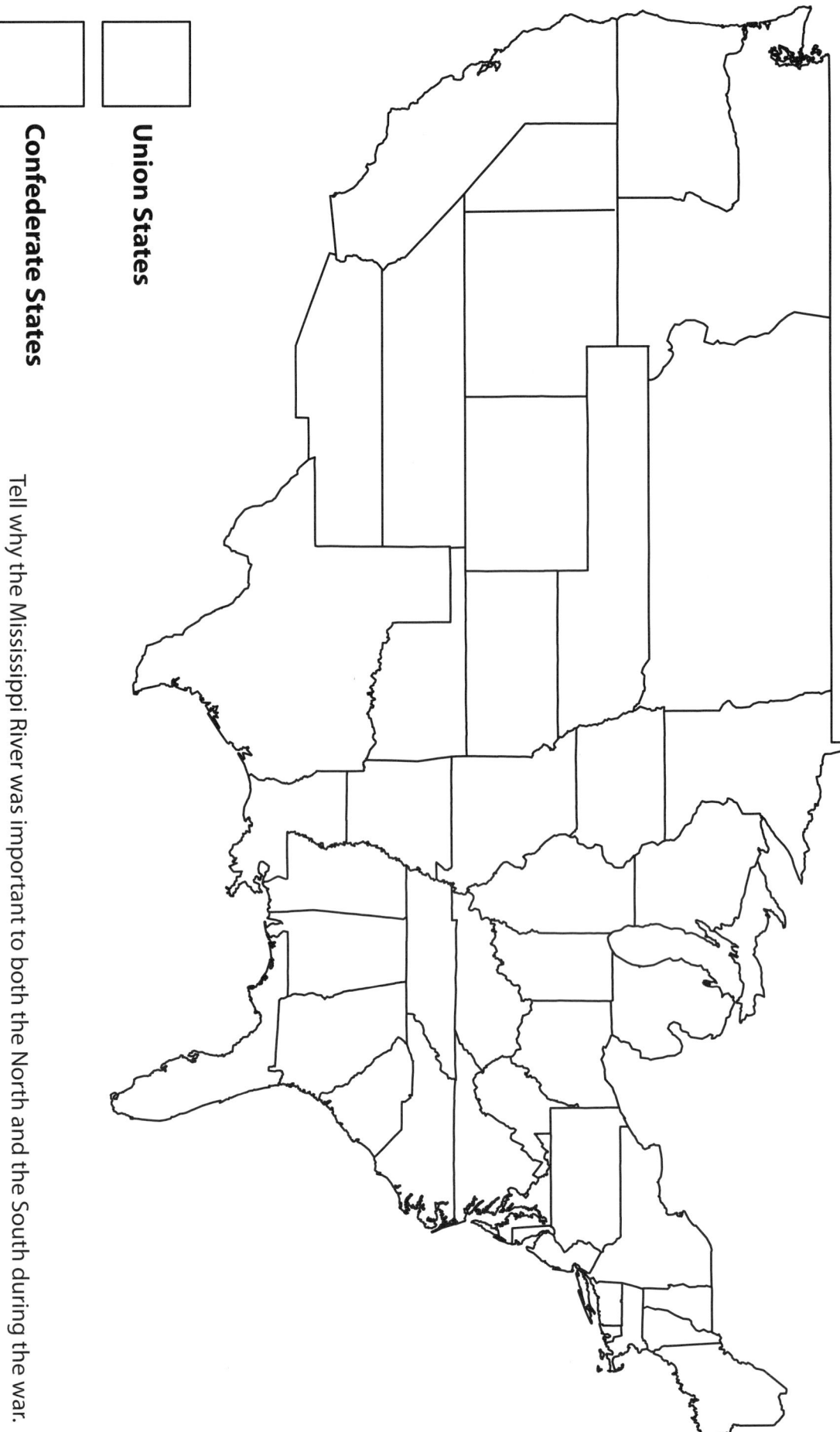

☐ **Union States**

☐ **Confederate States**

Tell why the Mississippi River was important to both the North and the South during the war.

At the beginning of the war, which side would you have predicted would win? Why?

Slavery

The issue of slavery was the leading cause of the Civil War. *Abolitionists* were people who felt that slavery should be ended. The life of a slave was completely controlled by his or her owner. It was against the law to educate slaves. Family and community life provided some relief from their cruel life. Some plantation owners thought that slaves who married and had children were easier to discipline and less likely to run away.

The conditions under which slaves lived varied widely. Some lived in the master's house, but most were housed in drafty, poorly furnished cabins. A slave might have only a bed of straw with a single blanket. A typical food allowance for one week might consist of one pound of saltpork and a quarter bushel of corn. Some slaves were allowed the time to supplement their diet by growing some of their own vegetables and fruit and raising chickens.

Project
Create menus for one week utilizing the normal food allowance for one slave.

Materials
- cookbooks
- paper
- pencil
- ingredients, utensils for one recipe

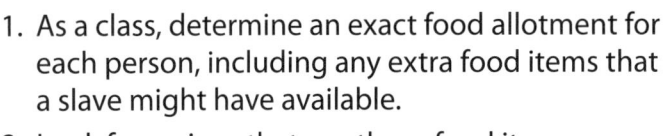

Directions
1. As a class, determine an exact food allotment for each person, including any extra food items that a slave might have available.
2. Look for recipes that use these food items, and plan a set of menus for one week.
3. Choose one recipe and prepare it.

Underground Railroad

There were many people in the North and South who risked their lives trying to help slaves escape from their owners. Some were white abolitionists and some were free blacks. A religious group named the Society of Friends, or Quakers, had begun to help slaves escape as early as 1786. By 1860, an elaborate system called the Underground Railroad was well established. The "railroad" was actually a system of escape routes through "depots," or safe houses.

At these safe-house locations, families were willing to hide runaway slaves, feed and clothe them as necessary, and help them on their way to the next safe stop along their escape route. The runaway slaves generally traveled by night and hid during daylight hours. The ultimate destination was usually Canada, where blacks could work freely and could vote. Operators of the Underground Railroad sometimes used disguised advertisements in newspapers to let prospective "riders" know of their existence.

Project
Research terms of the Underground Railroad.

Materials
- research materials
- poster board
- markers

Directions
On poster board, make a list of railroad-related terms used in the Underground Railroad to confuse slave chasers; i.e., "conductor" and "station." Explain what each meant. Compare your list with those of your classmates.

Term	Meaning
conductor	helpers along the routes

The Home Front

Underground Railroad

Knowledge of the Underground Railroad was passed along through word-of-mouth and coded messages, such as this one, appearing in a Chicago newspaper in 1844:

"The improved and splendid Locomotives, Clarkson and Lundy, with their trains fitted up in the best style of accommodation for passengers, will run their regular trips during the present season … Gentlemen and Ladies, who may wish to improve their health or circumstances, by a northern tour, are respectfully invited to give us their patronage."

Project
Design a poster to advertise the operation of an "Underground Railroad."

Materials
- poster board
- markers or crayons
- newspaper or magazine advertisements

Directions
1. Study advertisements and brainstorm ideas for ways of describing the Underground Railroad in advertising terms. Remember to disguise the true message of your advertisement.
2. Use poster board and markers or crayons to design ads.
3. Post finished advertisements on a bulletin board.

Aid Societies

People on the Union home front rallied to form aid societies that assisted in providing the many needs of the soldiers on the battlefront. Aid society members gathered canned and dried food, knitted socks, and made uniforms and underwear. They made bandages from any available material. They sold everything from baked goods to machinery to raise money to finance the war effort.

The food and clothing assembled were used to fill "comfort bags," which were sent to the troops. Although they didn't know who would receive the packages, aid society members and their children often added a personal note, encouraging the soldier and sending news from home.

Project
Prepare a "comfort bag" to send to a soldier on the battlefront.

Materials
- paper lunch bags
- magazines
- scissors
- items from home
- paper, pencils

Directions
1. Imagine you are a member of a modern-day aid society and are given the job of filling a comfort bag for a soldier. What items would you include?
2. Look through magazines and cut out pictures of things you would send. Add items brought from home. Write a personal note of encouragement and share some hometown news.
3. Meet in small discussion groups to share the contents of the comfort bag with group members. Explain the reason for your choices. Evaluate the choices of others.

Civil War Homes

By the time of the Civil War, homes began taking on the appearance and floor plans of homes we are familiar with today. Kitchens were separate from the dining room, with a cookstove and oven. The dining room became an important gathering place for the family. The parlor, similar to a living room, was another room where the family gathered for entertaining or for recreation. Parlors were often furnished with a large central table where the family worked or read together in the evenings.

Floors were covered with carpet, matting, or painted oilcloth. Wallpaper was frequently applied to the walls. Ceilings were often elaborately decorated. Houses were lit with candles or kerosene lamps. It was not uncommon for each family member to have his or her own bedroom.

Project

Choose one of the following Civil War home projects.

Diorama

Materials

- shoebox
- cardboard
- colored construction paper
- glue
- scissors
- research materials

Directions

1. Find illustrations, pictures, or recreations of the inside of a Civil War home. Choose the type of room you will make for your diorama.
2. Turn your shoebox on its side so that the top is now the front opening. Cover the outside and the inside of your shoebox with construction paper.
3. Using reference materials, create 3-dimensional objects out of cardboard and construction paper to place in your diorama. Objects can be hung from the "ceiling" with fishing line. Be as detailed as possible.
4. Write a description of what is in your diorama and glue it to the top. Display.

Then-and-Now Comparison Chart

What inventions have changed the way we live since Civil War times? Have these things made life better or worse?

Materials

- tagboard
- markers

Directions

1. On tagboard, draw a chart like the one below. Make a list of items we have in modern-day homes that Civil War homes did not (e.g., washing machines).
2. Under the Civil War Homes column, describe how these tasks were accomplished without modern technology.
3. Lastly, write whether you think the invention has made our lives better or worse, and why.

Civil War Homes	Modern Homes	Better or Worse?

Men's Clothing

By the time of the Civil War, great changes had taken place in clothing styles and construction. The invention of the sewing machine meant that clothes could be sold ready-made in stores. Standardized sewing patterns were available for home use.

Styles for men were less elaborate than they had been in earlier times. Men in the city wore dark suits with white shirts and ties. Stovepipe hats were popular, and many men carried pocket watches with chains and fobs. For home wear, men had loose jackets called smoking jackets.

Project
Dress like a businessman living in Civil War times.

Materials
- man's dress jacket
- wide black ribbon or bow tie
- white dress shirt
- stovepipe hat
- watch chain and fob

Directions
1. Follow the directions for making the stovepipe hat and the watch chain and fob.
2. Dress in suggested clothing.
3. Discuss Civil War dress compared to the way men dress today.

For the Teacher
Copy one Men's Clothing (page 11) and one Jewelry and Accessories (page 14) per student.

Men's Clothing

Stovepipe Hat
The stovepipe hat was a top hat that was popular throughout most of the nineteenth century. It could be made of many materials, from beaver skin to silk.

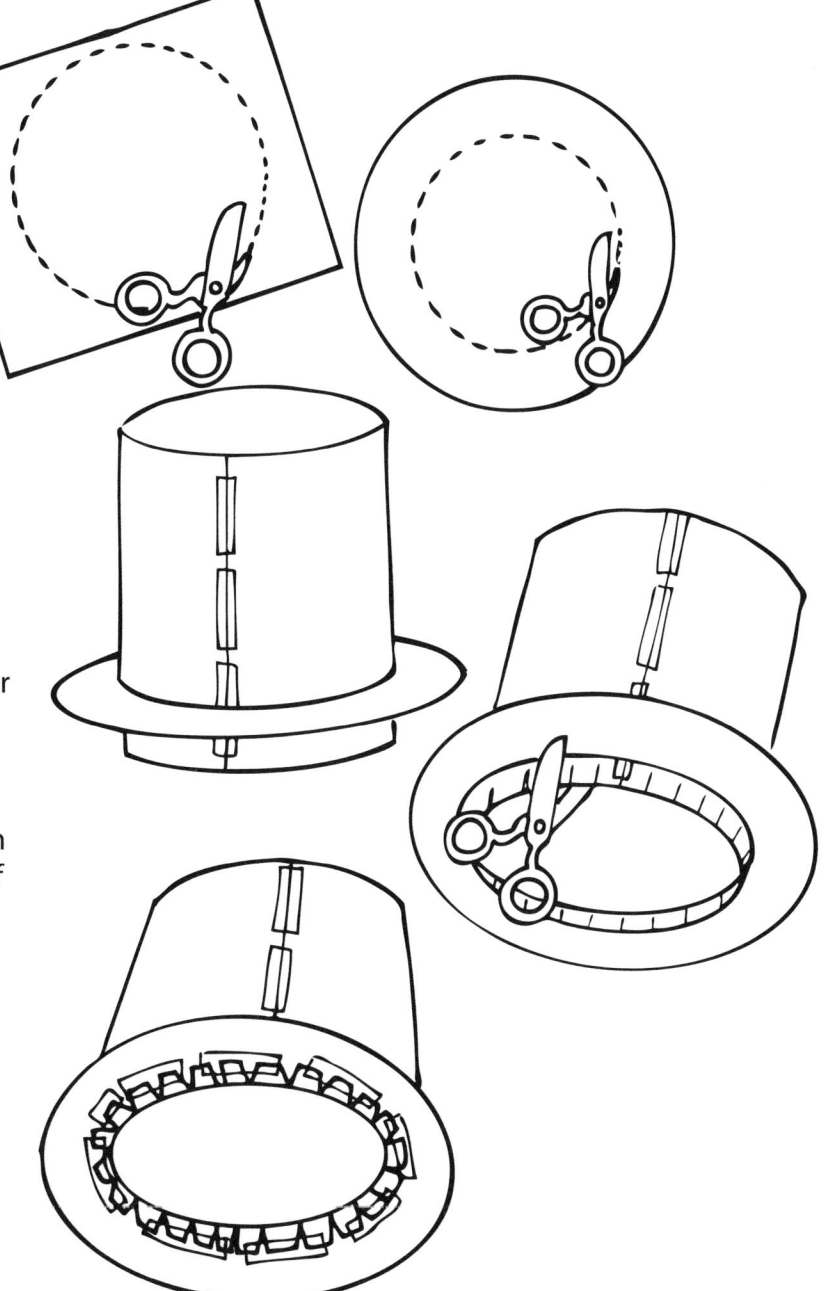

Materials
- black poster board
- black construction paper
- scissors
- tape

Directions
1. Cut a 12-inch (30.5 cm) circle from poster board to form base of hat.
2. Cut center out of the poster board circle, leaving 2 inches (5 cm) for the brim.
3. Cut a 12 x 27-inch (30.5 x 69-cm) rectangle of black construction paper for crown. Roll to form a column, adjusting to fit inside hat brim. Tape together.
4. Cut 1-inch (2.54-cm) slashes at 1-inch (2.54-cm) intervals around bottom of column. Fold up.
5. Tape folded tabs to underside of brim to form hat crown.

EP108 Civil War © Highsmith® Inc. 2007   The Home Front   11

Women's Clothing

Clothing for women in Civil War times could be very elaborate. Dresses were worn over large hoop skirts that were sometimes so wide that a woman might have difficulty going through doors. Several layers of petticoats were worn under the skirt. Women also wore corsets, which bound their waists to unnaturally small sizes. Women accessorized their ensembles with gloves, jewelry, and elaborate hats.

Many types of fabric were used for clothing, but cotton was the most common. Manufacturing methods were so improved that cotton fabrics could have many different textures, colors, and prints.

Project
Create a hoop skirt and bonnet to be worn as part of a Civil War ensemble.

Materials
- hula hoop
- measuring tape
- fabric
- needle, thread
- elastic
- long, full skirt
- poke bonnet
- gloves
- scissors

Directions
1. Measure circumference of hula hoop. Cut fabric to that length, adding 2 inches (5 cm).
2. Sew ends of fabric together. Fold over the top edge 1 inch (2.54 cm) to form casing.
3. Stitch, leaving a 1- to 2-inch (2.5- to 5-cm) opening to insert elastic.
4. Wrap bottom edge up over hula hoop and sew into place.
5. Wear long skirt over the hoop skirt and add accessories.
4. Discuss the difference between Civil War clothing and the dresses of today.

For the Teacher
Copy one Women's Clothing (page 13) per student.

Women's Clothing

Poke Bonnet
Poke bonnets were one type of hat worn by women in Civil War times. They were often elaborately decorated with ribbons, flowers, and feathers.

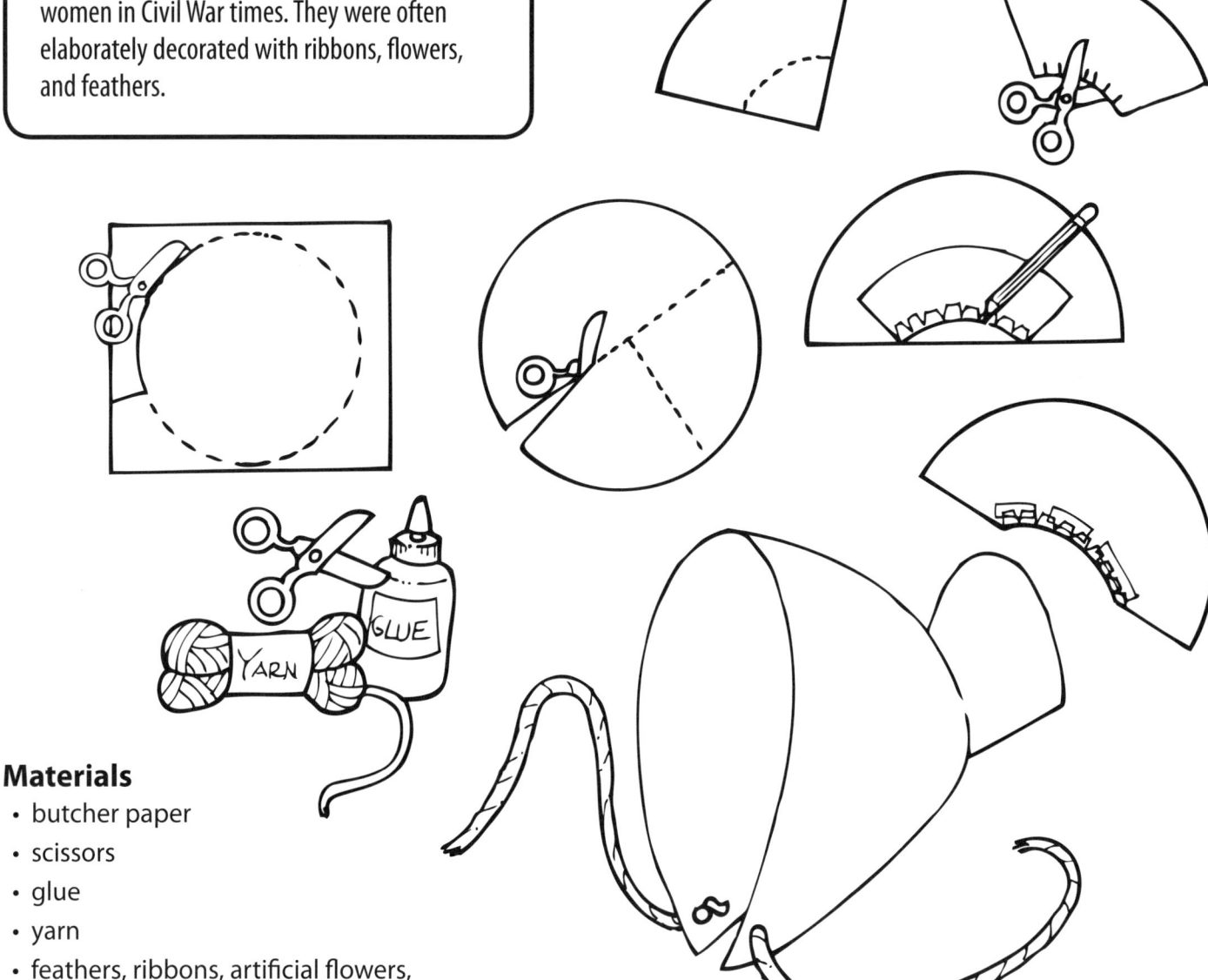

Materials
- butcher paper
- scissors
- glue
- yarn
- feathers, ribbons, artificial flowers, assorted trims

Directions
1. Cut a 22-inch (56-cm) circle from butcher paper.
2. Fold circle in half and cut to make two half-circles.
3. Cut one of half-circles in half again. Discard one section. Cut remaining quarter-circle as shown in diagram.
4. Make 1-inch (2.54 cm) slashes at intervals as shown. Fold back.
5. Lay quarter-circle on top of half-circle as shown and trace a curved cutting line. Cut away excess paper.
6. Tape folded edges of quarter-circle along cut edge of half-circle, curving larger piece to make a brim.
7. Cut slits at each corner and insert lengths of yarn to tie bonnet under chin.
8. Decorate bonnet by gluing on selected trims.

EP108 Civil War © Highsmith® Inc. 2007

The Home Front

Jewelry and Accessories

Men and women of the Civil War era embellished their daily dress with jewelry and other types of ornaments. Women carried fans and drawstring handbags, similar to handbags of today. They wore *snoods*, or crocheted hair nets, to cover their hair during the day. Men attached their pocket watches to chains from which dangled decorative baubles or charms, called *fobs*. Men during the Civil War era carried their watches in a special pocket just below the waistband of their suit. The chain and fobs were outside the pocket.

Mourning jewelry of all kinds was worn, often made of jet (polished coal), wood, or even hair from the deceased. Also popular were cameos, set into rings, necklaces, and earrings.

Project
Make Civil War-era jewelry and accessories.

Watch and Fob

Materials
- aluminum foil
- poster board
- paper clips
- scissors
- hole punch
- large needle

Directions
1. Cut a 2-inch (5-cm) circle from poster board and cover with aluminum foil to make a watch. Punch a hole in circle.
2. Cut small shapes from poster board and cover with foil. These may be decorative or represent an object. With a needle, poke a hole in each one.
3. Link several paper clips together to form a chain, attaching cutouts as the chain is formed by pushing sharp end of paper clip through the hole in the ornament.
4. Attach the "watch" to one end of the chain with paper clip.

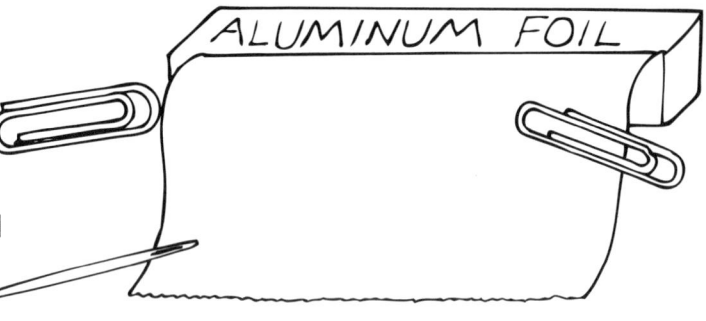

14 The Home Front

Jewelry and Accessories

Hair Jewelry

Human hair, woven and braided into necklaces, bracelets, earrings, and watch chains, served as mementoes of friends and relatives who had died. Sometimes hair from several family members was interwoven.

Materials

- yarn in various colors

Directions

1. Cut several strands of yarn, all the same color or in various colors.
2. Experiment with weaving and braiding to find a pleasing pattern.
3. Fashion a bracelet or necklace from the braided length of yarn.

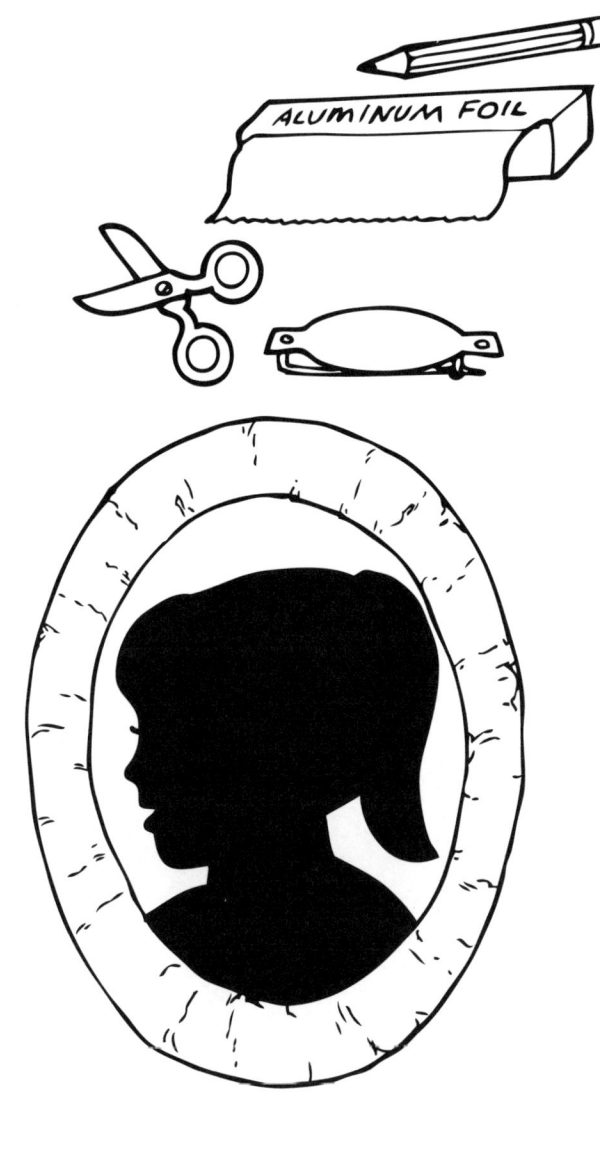

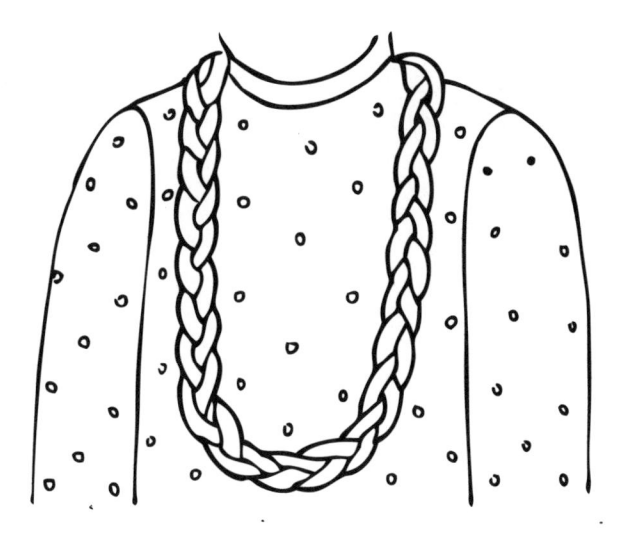

Cameos

A cameo is a gem carved with a figure raised in relief.

Materials

- poster board oval, 3 inches (7.6 cm) long
- aluminum foil
- construction paper oval (other than white), slightly smaller than poster board
- white construction paper
- pencil
- scissors
- tacky glue
- pin back

Directions

1. Cover poster board oval with aluminum foil.
2. Glue white construction paper oval to foil-covered oval.
3. On colored construction paper, draw the profile of a face to fit inside construction paper oval. Cut out and glue to white construction paper.
4. Glue pin back to back-side of foil-covered oval.

Photography

When the war began in 1861, photography had been in existence only 22 years. Thousands of newly-enlisted soldiers and volunteers with "war fever" rushed to have their portraits taken. They donned whatever clothing and weapons they had available without waiting for their official uniforms to be issued. The poses often looked stiff, the faces expressionless. This was due, in part, to the 10-second exposure time and the fact that their head was placed in metal clamps to prevent them from moving and blurring the picture. To give the illusion of an outdoor shot, the photographer painted backdrops featuring outdoor scenes.

Photography on the battlefield was also very difficult. It would take two photographers to prepare the chemicals and glass plates. The exposure of the plate and development of the photograph had to be done in just minutes in a wagon darkroom. The glass plates were fragile and hard to take care of on the battlefield.

Mathew B. Brady is probably the most well-known Civil War photographer. His corps of photographers took to the battlefields to document the war. Many photographs are attributed to Brady that were actually taken by his traveling photographers. In 1862, Brady displayed some of his most explicit photographs in a show titled "The Dead of Antietam." These photos shocked the nation and became known as the first photo-documentation of a war.

Project
Compare the photo-documentation of the Civil War with more recent documentation of war.

Materials
- notebook paper
- markers

Directions
1. Brainstorm a list of ways we find out about news, world events, war, etc., in modern day. Compare this list to the ways the public found out about what was happening on the battlefields during the Civil War. How have things changed? Do you think the information we receive now changes our view of war?
2. Write a few paragraphs detailing your thoughts.
3. Then, photocopy a picture of yourself (not smiling if possible!) and place it in the Photo Frame. Decorate the frame and post it next to your thoughts on a classroom bulletin board.

For the Teacher
Copy one Photo Frame (page 17) per student. Feature all of the finished framed "photographs" and essays in a classroom display.

Photo Frame

EP108 Civil War © Highsmith® Inc. 2007   **The Home Front**   17

Bank Notes

The banking system during this period was chaotic throughout the North and the South. Every state, many towns, banks, and even stores issued their own currency. To finance the war effort, the South issued Federal bonds—loans in the form of paper money—that the Confederate government promised to repay, with interest, after the war was won. The debt was never repaid.

By 1865, inflation in the south reached 9,000 percent. A Confederate "dollar" was worth barely more than a penny. Small fish sold for $20, chickens were $10 each. A Union private was paid only $13 a month. A Confederate got $2 less. Bonuses were paid for enlisting and re-enlisting.

Project
Set up a Civil War store and spend paper currency.

Materials
- bank notes
- plastic food
- food pictures cut from magazines

Directions
1. Set up a Civil War store with plastic food items and pictures of food cut from magazines.
2. Price the items in the store. Keep in mind the inflation of the era.
3. Decide which class members are bankers, shopkeepers, Union soldiers, and Confederate soldiers. Determine how long the soldiers have served in the army and whether or not they deserve a bonus for re-enlisting.
4. Bankers pay each soldier the amount due.
5. Soldiers go shopping with the earned pay. Return everything to the store and assign different roles.

For the Teacher
Copy one Bank Notes page (19) per student.

18   **The Home Front**   EP108 Civil War © Highsmith® Inc. 2007

Bank Notes

EP108 Civil War © Highsmith® Inc. 2007 　　　　　**The Home Front**　19

Uniforms

Combat participants in the Civil War, from both the North and the South, dressed in a wide variety of uniforms, depending on the unit or regiment to which the soldiers or sailors belonged. Most Union soldiers were issued light blue pants and a long, dark blue jacket, as well as a dark blue kepi cap.

The official uniform for a Confederate soldier was a long gray shirt with light blue trousers and a gray flannel overcoat. Some wore shirts and pants of homespun cotton, dyed brown with walnut shells. Most wound up being dressed in scratchy wool shirts and roughly made pants.

The aid societies and others on both home fronts (North and South) were faced with the prospects of making uniforms for the fighting troops from limited supplies. They had to be imaginative with their use of materials, recycling such things as curtains into articles of clothing that were useful to soldiers on the war front.

Scores of regiments equipped themselves locally, wearing uniforms of their own design, financed by fund-raising drives or local businessmen. The dwindling supply of uniforms, particularly among the *Rebel* (Confederate) forces, led to soldiers wearing whatever uniform they could get their hands on. Often they stripped a dead soldier for his shirt, trousers, shoes, and other articles of clothing. By the middle of the war, mismatched troops were a common sight, with deadly consequences when soldiers did not know who they were fighting on the battlefield.

Project
Use recycled items to create a new article of clothing.

Materials
- discarded cloth items: sheets, rags, towels, pot holders, fabric
- masking tape, thread, string, rope, cardboard, shoe boxes, and other recyclable materials

Directions
Use the materials provided to "recycle" the available items to create a new article of clothing such as shoes, hat, belt, or other item that might be worn by a soldier.

Tents and Shelters

Since most battles in the Civil War were fought in the warmer climate of the South, a tent was a soldier's home for three seasons of the year. A variety of tents appeared at the outset of the war. Some units came with candy-striped tents. Others showed up with nothing at all. Canvas tents, shaped like a small house, were popular, but also expensive and cumbersome to pitch and carry. They eventually became shelters for hospital patients and officers. The Sibley tent resembled a teepee, a tall cone of canvas supported by a center pole. Often more than 20 men inhabited a single tent, their heads at the outer rim and feet at the center pole. The dog tent, shaped like an upside-down V with rifles serving as poles, was the version most used by the soldiers. Two men each carried half, and they buttoned the halves together at night.

Project

Erect tents and create a mini war front encampment.

Materials

- small sticks or tent stakes
- dowels, broom handles, or long branches
- sheets or other large pieces of fabric
- scissors
- tape
- rope
- hammer

Directions

1. Divide into groups of four.
2. Discuss the supplies needed to construct a tent. Use the material list as a guide. Assign each group member an item to supply.
3. Erect the tent shelters on a grassy area on the playground.
4. Evaluate the ease with which the tents were erected; how comfortable they might be to sleep in; and how effective they would be as protection against the weather.
5. Conduct some camp activities while the tents are constructed. Play games (see Camp Recreation, page 34) or eat a simple meal (see Battlefield Food, page 38).

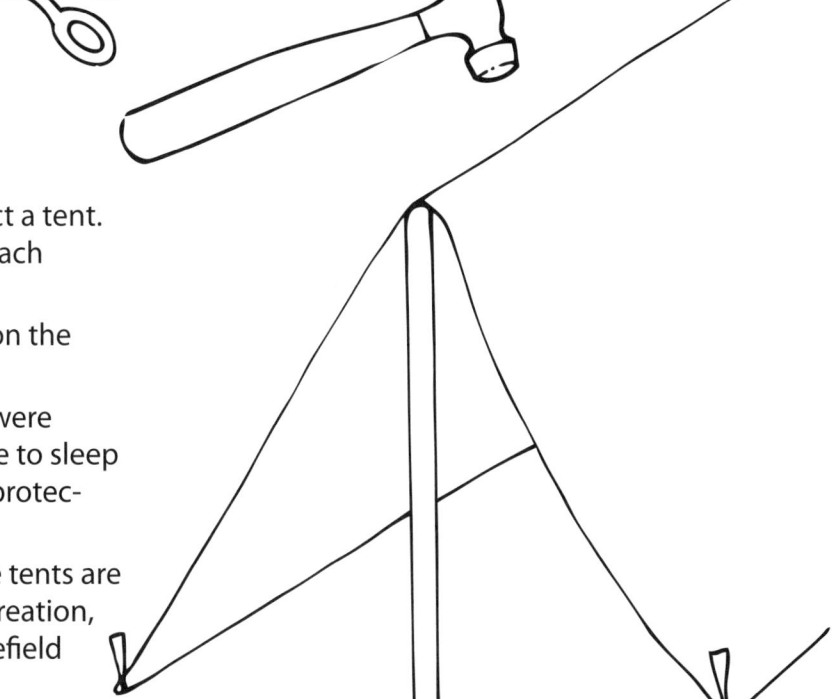

Soldiers' Supplies

The call to arms and initial excitement of the war sent thousands of men shopping for their own supplies. Newspapers tempted new recruits with advertisements featuring the latest inventions and gadgets intended to make life on the war front more convenient.

Pocketed belts, bulletproof vests, mess kettles, and even a portable 9-pound (4 kg) stove (cost: $6) were among the supplies offered for sale. Once purchased, they did not last long. Long hours of marching and difficult conditions forced soldiers to abandon these "luxuries." A bedroll, knapsack, and canteen were the only items a soldier could realistically carry.

Project
Construct some of the supplies sold through newspaper advertisements at the outset of the Civil War.

Materials
- Soldiers' Supplies page
- materials as listed for each project
- scissors
- glue
- stapler

For the Teacher
Copy one Soldiers' Supplies page (23) per student. Cut apart the project cards.

Directions
1. Review each project on the Soldiers' Supplies page and choose one to complete.
2. Display your finished project and demonstrate its use for the class.

Soldiers' Supplies

Money Belt

Materials
- butcher paper
- blunt needle
- yarn
- scissors
- markers
- stapler

Directions
Cut the butcher paper into a strip 12 x 24 inches (30.5 x 61 cm). Fold one long side up 5 inches (12.7 cm). Stitch the ends closed. Stitch at intervals to create pockets. Staple a 4-foot (1.22 m) length of yarn above pockets to tie around waist. Fold the top flap down 1 inch (2.54 cm). Label each pocket with something a soldier might have carried.

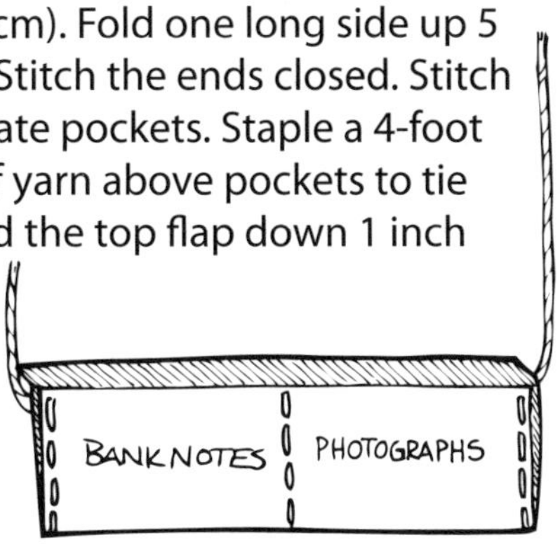

Mess Kettle

Materials
- assorted boxes, bucket, bottles, jars, paper plates, cups, and plastic utensils

Directions
Start with a large box or bucket and fill it with jars, plates, and other kitchen items. The items should all stack inside neatly.

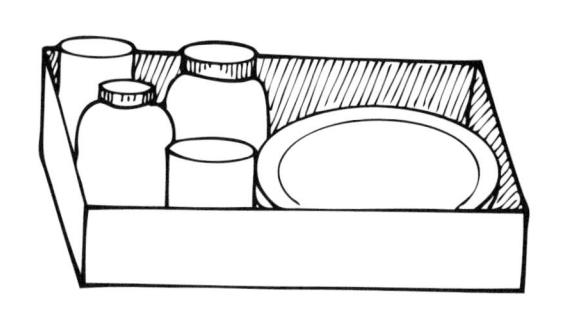

Canteen

Materials
- two sturdy paper plates
- stapler
- cloth strips
- brown paint
- sponge

Directions
Sponge paint the paper plates on the rounded side. Staple the plates together, painted side out. Leave an opening at the top. Staple a cloth strip to each side of the "canteen."

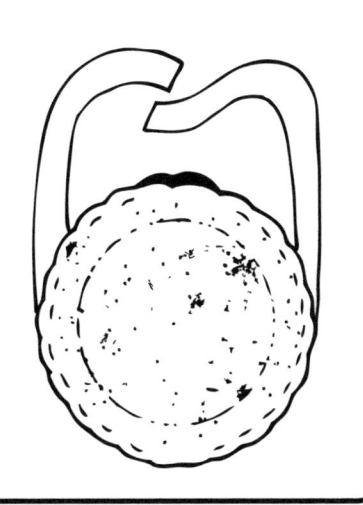

Bulletproof Vest

Materials
- 2 large grocery bags
- scissors
- newspapers
- stapler

Directions
Cut the bags up the front. Create neck and arm openings. Place a layer of newspaper between the two bags and staple the bags together.

EP108 Civil War © Highsmith® Inc. 2007   The War Front   23

Haversacks

Soldiers didn't have what we commonly refer to today as backpacks. They were carrying their tents on their backs. However, they did need some sort of bag or carryall for their personal items. So, a 1-foot-square (.30-m) canvas bag, with a strap to hang over the shoulder, called a haversack, was part of their military gear. It had a waterproof lining that could be removed for washing. Still, this did not prevent the sack from becoming greasy and foul-smelling between washings, considering all the contents that had to be carried in it.

Haversacks were designed to carry personal items that included a man's housewife (see page 25), soap and towel, toothbrush, comb, money, Bible, letters, newspaper, cards and dice, and three days' rations (uncooked daily food allowances issued to soldiers that they were required to prepare on their own). Rations for three days were important if the soldiers were going to be moving from one location to another.

Project
Create a "haversack" like Civil War soldiers carried.

Materials
- muslin fabric
- two large buttons
- needle and thread
- scissors
- some personal items from home as mentioned above

Directions
1. For the sack, cut a piece of fabric 13 x 31 inches (33 x 79 cm).
2. For the strap, cut another piece of fabric 2 inches (5 cm) wide by 36 inches (.91 m) long.
3. Turn up a short side of the sack fabric about 12 inches (30.5 cm). One-half inch (1.25 cm) from the edge, begin sewing the first side. When you reach the last two inches (5 cm), insert the strap fabric and continue sewing the side, including the strap. Repeat for the other side. Turn inside out.
4. Cut a slit, evenly positioned, near each corner of the remaining flap of the fabric.
5. Turn down and mark the position where each button should be sewn. Sew buttons in place.
6. Fill your "haversack" with personal items you brought from home.

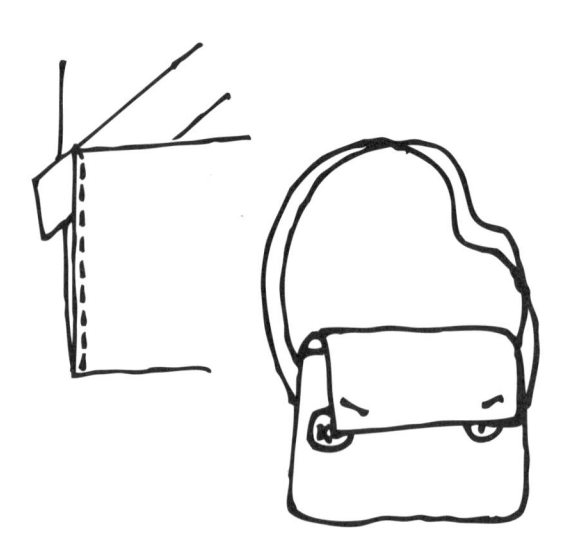

24 **The War Front**

"Housewife"

Newly enlisted soldiers, tempted by the large variety of items offered for sale, often took heavy packs along with them when they joined their company. It wasn't long before these "extras" were abandoned. Veteran soldiers traveled lightly, carrying few extra items. One of the most important was called a *housewife,* a small sewing kit stocked with needle, thread, and buttons.

A "housewife" was essential on the war front. Men who had never used a needle and thread before became experts at patching rips, mending tears, and sewing on buttons. Replacement clothing was a rarity, particularly in the southern states. Soldiers had to make do with the clothes on their backs.

Project
Make a "housewife" and learn the fundamentals of sewing.

Materials
- needles
- thread
- scissors
- fabric remnants
- buttons

Directions
1. Practice threading the needle and tying a knot in the thread.
2. Cut one large rectangle and one smaller square of fabric to be sewn on as a pocket.
3. Place the square on the larger rectangle and use a running stitch on three sides to sew it in place.
4. Practice sewing on several buttons and some small patches, as well.

Medicine

At the beginning of the war, the U.S. Army had only around 100 physicians, or surgeons as they were called. Many of these surgeons had only gone through 1 to 2 years and sometimes as little as 13 weeks of required medical training. The medical field at the time held many misconceptions, including the belief that pus coming from a wound was good sign. It was, in fact, the sign of a bacterial infection that could kill a soldier.

Surgeons also did not have much medical equipment. They lacked tools such as a stethoscopes, microscopes, and syringes. They used morphine as a pain killer and administered it by rubbing it directly into wounds, or sometimes through opium pills. Many soldiers came home addicted to opium because surgeons were unaware of its addictive properties.

Amputation was the most common surgery performed during the Civil War. Although the procedure was unsophisticated compared to today's methods, amputation saved many lives during the war.

Project
Make a diary of a Civil War surgeon or a wounded soldier.

Materials
- 11 x 17-inch (28 x 43-cm) piece of brown construction paper
- notebook paper
- stapler

Directions
1. Fold an 11 x 17-inch (28 x 43-cm) piece of brown construction paper in half. Insert a few pieces of notebook paper in the middle of the construction paper. Staple together at the fold to form a book.

2. Choose one of the following prompts to create a diary.
   - Pretend you are a Civil War surgeon. Write diary entries for a week in your life tending to the sick and wounded on the battlefield. Fill in your diary with your thoughts, fears, and accomplishments.
   - Pretend you are a wounded soldier on the battlefield. Are you from the North or South? What is your ailment? Fill in your diary with a week's worth of entries.

4. Compare your diaries with your classmates. You may wish to role-play the entries by reading them out loud.

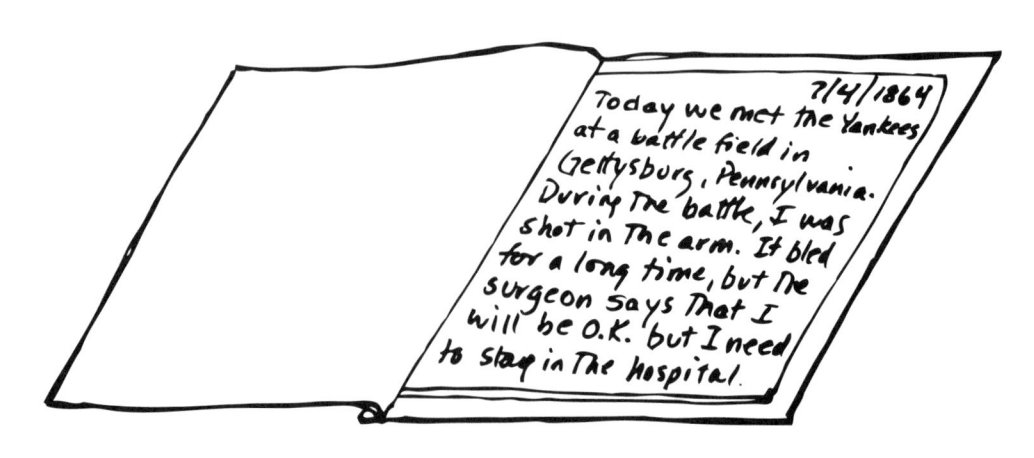

Clara Barton

Medical care for the men wounded on Civil War battlefields was primitive. Medical equipment was often not cleaned between uses. Infection in wounds was common because there were no antibiotics. Many men died from infectious diseases caused by poor sanitation.

Clara Barton, a government clerk from North Oxford, Massachusetts, began to carry supplies to soldiers and to nurse wounded men on the battlefield. Called an "Angel of the Battlefield," her work attracted national attention and appreciation. In 1881, Clara Barton founded the American Red Cross. After the Civil War, she formed an organization to search for missing men.

Project
Gather equipment to be used in a medical kit on a Civil War battlefield.

Materials
- shoebox
- muslin
- poster board
- scissors
- markers
- black tempera paint and brush
- needles and thread, small pliers (optional)

Directions
1. Paint the shoebox with black paint.
2. Make bandages by cutting muslin into 3-inch (7.5-cm) strips. Roll tightly and store in box.
3. Cut a small handsaw shape from poster board. Paint or embellish with markers.
4. Decide what other kinds of equipment might be in a medical kit (small pliers to remove bullets, needles and thread for stitches, etc.).

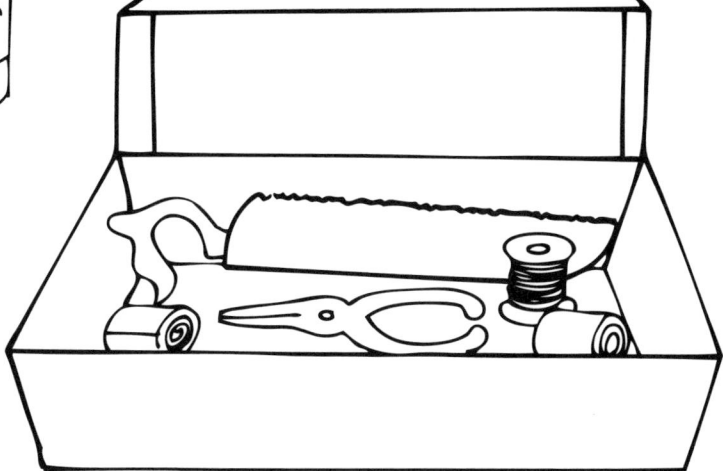

Extended Activity
Clara Barton learned of the International Committee of the Red Cross while visiting Switzerland and became the first president of the American branch in 1881.
- Research the history of the Red Cross organization.
- Look through newspapers and magazines to determine what things the Red Cross does today.

Camp Portraits

Traveling photographers followed the troops from one battle site and encampment to the next, recording the events of the war. Soldiers paid about one dollar each for portraits to send home to loved ones. One of the first methods of photographic print was called a *daguerreotype*, named for Louis Daguerre, who perfected the process of exposing a silver copper plate to chemicals to create permanent images with outstanding detail.

In another method, an individual's photo image was printed from a glass negative onto a paper card. These miniature portraits, used as calling cards, were known as *carte de visite*. A soldier could purchase a dozen carte de visite for three to five dollars.

Project
Create two types of camp portraits.

Materials
- Camp Portraits Project Page
- materials for each project, as listed

Directions
1. Review the directions on the Camp Portraits Project Page.
2. Divide into cooperative groups to paint the backdrops and form groups for regimental pictures.

For the Teacher
Copy one Camp Portraits Project Page (29) per student.

Camp Portraits Project Page

Daguerreotype

Materials
- butcher paper
- tempera paint
- paintbrushes
- camera with black and white film
- uniforms (see page 20)
- Civil War reference books

Directions
1. Review photographs from Civil War encampments.
2. Paint a large mural backdrop featuring weaponry, tents, landscape, and other images representative of camp life.
3. Dress up in class-created uniforms and have "regiment" pictures taken against the backdrop.

Carte de Visite

Materials
- six index cards
- small personal photograph (school portrait size)
- glue
- photocopy machine

Directions
1. Make six photocopies of each individual photo.
2. Glue a photocopy to each index card to create six carte de visite.
3. Include a signature and a brief message from the "war front."
4. Trade the carte de visite with classmates.

Regimental Flags

When the various troops marched off to war, they carried with them the colors and insignia of their native state. Some flags carried their unit's nickname, like the "Bartow Yankee Killers" or "Floyd Rangers." The flags were not uniform in design. They were sewn from silk, cotton, and wool. Some were made using the fabric of wedding dresses or grain sacks.

Despite it being the most dangerous post, men would vie with one another to carry the regimental banners into battle. As soon as one color bearer fell, another rushed to take his place. A dozen or more men might fall carrying the colors in a single battle.

Project
Work in cooperative groups to design and make a regimental flag.

Materials
- basic art supplies such as construction paper scraps, scissors, glue, stapler
- additional materials as requested by cooperative groups

Directions
1. Form cooperative groups. Discuss and make some group decisions:
   - Are you Confederate or Union?
   - Which state are you from?
   - What is your troop's nickname?
   - What are your troop colors?
2. Design a flag for your regiment. Decide on the material from which it will be made, then assign people to locate in class or bring from home the necessary materials.
3. Construct your flag and display it in the classroom.

Buglers and Drummers

Most soldiers were between 18 and 29 years of age. Sixteen- and 17-year-olds who wanted to enlist wrote the number "18" on slips of paper and put them in their shoes. When asked by a recruiting officer how old they were, they could say, "over eighteen." Ten- and 12-year-olds often were placed in the supposedly non-combatant roles of buglers and drummers. The youngest soldier of the war, aged nine, joined as a musician.

Drum rolls and bugle calls stood for certain orders. There were 15 general drum rolls and 26 bugle calls, and more for skirmishes. Forgetting their meaning could prove disastrous for a fighting man.

For the Teacher

Project
Create and respond to commands issued by drum and whistle rhythms.

Materials
- drum and drumstick, or object on which to beat a rhythm
- whistle or recorder
- chalkboard, chalk

Directions
1. As a class, create five to 10 drum and whistle commands. For example:
   - Three drum beats: Step forward five paces.
   - Two whistle blasts and two drum beats: Lie down.
2. Spend some time memorizing the commands and their meanings.
3. Head outside to the "battlefield." Choose two students to be drummer and bugler. "Play" a command and ask classroom troops to follow. Allow time between each one. Change buglers and drummers occasionally. Evaluate your success in following the commands!

Music

In the military encampments and on the home front, each side rallied around music that became identified with their cause. Every camp had a band that featured instruments the soldiers carried from home and any instruments they made from materials on hand. Sounds of fiddles, harmonicas, and banjos filled the air when weary soldiers gathered around a campfire. Those who didn't have instruments whistled tunes and sang.

Larger companies formed musical groups that performed for civilian and military personnel.

For the Teacher

Project
Gather around a campfire and play some Civil War music.

Materials
- brown butcher paper
- masking tape
- Song Sheet
- tape or record player
- recordings of the songs listed
- musical instruments

Directions
1. Create a campfire by rolling and taping brown butcher paper into logs.
2. Clear an area for the "campfire" and stack the logs in the center.
3. Copy one Song Sheet (page 33) per student.
4. Bring musical instruments to the campfire and have students play, sing, or whistle along with the songs on the record or tape player.

Extended Activity
Many songs have an interesting history. "The Battle Hymn of the Republic" was originally a poem written by Julia Ward Howe, a citizen who was inspired after viewing a grand review of the troops in Washington, D.C. Research the history of other patriotic and Civil War songs.

The War Front

Song Sheet

North

Union musical favorites included:
"When Johnny Comes Marching Home," "The Battle Hymn of the Republic," "John Brown's Body," "Rally Round the Flag," and "Tenting on the Old Campground"

The Battle Hymn of the Republic

Mine eyes have seen the glory of the coming of the Lord;
He is trampling out the vintage where the grapes of wrath are stored;
He has loosed the fateful lightning of His terrible swift sword;
His truth is marching on!
Glory! Glory! Hallelujah!
Glory! Glory! Hallelujah!
Glory! Glory! Hallelujah!
His truth is marching on.

When Johnny Comes Marching Home Again

When Johnny comes marching home again,
Hurrah! Hurrah!
We'll give him a hearty welcome then,
Hurrah! Hurrah!
The men will cheer, the boys will shout
The ladies they will all turn out,
And we'll all feel gay when
Johnny comes marching home.

South

Confederate musical favorites included:
"Bonnie Blue Flag," "Home Sweet Home," "Dixie," "Pop Goes the Weasel," "Shoo Fly Shoo," "Goober Peas"

Dixie

I wish I was in the land of cotton,
Old times there are not forgotten,
Look away, look away, look away Dixie land.
In Dixie land, where I was born in
Early on one frosty mornin',
Look away, look away, look away Dixie land.
Then I wish I was in Dixie,
Hooray! Hooray!
In Dixie land I'll take my stand,
To live and die in Dixie,
Away, away, away down south in Dixie.
Away, away, away down south in Dixie.

Goober Peas

Sitting by the roadside on a summer day,
Chatting with my messmates passing time away;
Lying in the shadow underneath the trees,
Goodness, how delicious, eating goober peas.
Peas, peas, peas, peas, eating goober peas,
Goodness, how delicious, eating goober peas.

Camp Recreation

For every day spent in battle, Yankees and Rebels passed weeks and months fighting other enemies: heat and cold, hunger, poor sanitation, disease, and the monotony of drill, training, and camp life. Camp diversions included music and conversation around a campfire, checkers, chess, and card games. Some took up carving as a hobby, making poker chips, whistles, and small figurines out of wood and animal bone.

More active pastimes included wrestling and foot races, sometimes with wheelbarrows or over hurdles. Cannon balls were used as bowling balls with cricket pins as their targets. Baseball—a different version than today's—was often played.

For the Teacher

Project
Participate in indoor and outdoor camp recreational activities

Materials
- checker and chessboard and pieces
- playing cards
- wood blocks
- rubber ball
- shoeboxes
- baseball
- hurdles
- glue

Directions
1. Set up three indoor recreation stations:
   - checkers and chess
   - card games
   - wood construction—wood blocks and glue
2. Set up three outdoor recreation stations:
   - bowling—10 upended shoe boxes, rubber ball
   - hurdles
   - baseball diamond and equipment
3. Plan a day (or as time permits) to participate in these activities. Students may rotate through all areas or choose those of interest.

Newspapers

Much of the news from the war front consisted of rumors. The most dependable source of information was the newspaper. Even the spies on both sides turned to enemy newspapers for information. The North had more paper mills and printing presses, and therefore had more newspapers and reporters.

As the war progressed, paper became scarce, particularly in the Confederate states. They wrote on scraps of paper. When they ran out of newsprint, they printed on the back of patterned wallpaper, brown wrapping paper, and thin tissue paper. When supplies of ink were gone, they used shoe polish. By the end of the war, only 20 Southern newspapers remained.

Project
Create a newspaper using different kinds of paper.

Materials
- wallpaper samples
- tissue paper
- brown bags or wrapping paper
- shoe polish
- paper bowl
- toothpicks
- butcher paper

Directions
1. Select paper—wallpaper, tissue paper, or brown paper.
2. Pour shoe polish into paper bowl. Use toothpick dipped in shoe polish to write three or four sentences reporting events on the battlefield or home front.

For the Teacher
Mount all reports on butcher paper to create a giant newspaper.

Correspondents

In the first few months of the war, the Pony Express carried news reports. However, shortly after, reporters traveling with troops were able to send their reports via telegraph. Their average salary was $25 per week. The invention of photography 22 years earlier made the Civil War the first war to be recorded with photo-journalism. Some newspapers also paid illustrators to sketch battlefield scenes and impressions.

Small towns couldn't afford to pay correspondents. They filled their newspapers with letters mailed from soldiers, and reprints of stories from larger papers.

Project
Create a war correspondent's sketch book.

Materials
- pens and pencils
- drawing paper
- butcher paper

Directions
1. Use pens, pencils, and drawing paper to make sketches of Civil War battle or war front scenes.
2. Mount sketches on butcher paper to make a bulletin board display. Articles describing the sketches may also be included.

The War Front

Medal of Honor

Courageous acts abounded on the battlefield. The governments of the opposing forces devised ways to honor this bravery. Confederate fighting forces were recognized by a Roll of Honor published after every battle. The Union, which had had no military decorations since the Revolutionary War, established the Medal of Honor in 1861, with Congressional approval, to recognize acts of bravery. The approval caused much debate among U.S. citizens and politicians because many people considered medals to be symbols of European monarchies. More than 1,000 Medals of Honor were awarded to Union soldiers, including at least 21 issued to black soldiers. A Confederate Medal of Honor was never issued due to disagreements and lack of finances.

Project
Create a paper replica of a Civil War Medal of Honor.

Materials
- yellow, white, and blue construction paper
- cardboard
- scissors
- tape and glue
- wide blue ribbon

Directions
1. Cut out the medal pattern and use it to cut a star out of cardboard and a star out of yellow construction paper. Paste the construction paper star over the cardboard. Draw a design on the star to represent an act of bravery or a good deed of one of your classmates.
2. Use the top of the medal pattern to cut an octagon out of cardboard and another out of blue construction paper. Glue the blue paper on top of the cardboard. Draw 13 small white stars on the blue octagon. Cut a 2-inch length of ribbon. Attach the star to the octagon by gluing the ribbon to the back of each shape.
3. Measure enough ribbon to hang the medal around your neck. Glue the ends of the ribbon to the back of the octagon to create a neck strap.

For the Teacher
Copy one Medal of Honor pattern (below) per student. When students finish the project, hold a Medal Ceremony and present medals to their recipients.

EP108 Civil War © Highsmith® Inc. 2007

The War Front   37

Battlefield Food

Near-famine conditions hampered troops on both sides. Union soldiers lived mainly on salt pork, bread, beans, and coffee, supplemented with cakes and pies bought from *sutlers*, peddlers who followed troops from camp to camp. Aid societies in the North sent thousands of boxes containing smoked meats, pies, dried fruits, and jams. Most of the food spoiled before it reached the troops.

Confederate supplies were not as plentiful. They suffered through days with no rations. Meals were fried in grease and stomach ailments abounded. *Hardtack*, rock-hard flour-and-water biscuits, were the main staple, but were so infested with insects that soldiers came to call them "worm-castles."

Project
Simulate a battlefield and dine on Civil War soldiers' rations.

Materials
- Battlefield Food Project Page
- hot plate
- bowls
- plastic spoons
- ingredients as listed in each recipe

Directions
1. Divide into Union and Confederate camps. Gather ingredients and supplies needed to complete each recipe.
2. Set up a "chow" line in each camp.
3. Serve the meals and "coffee."

For the Teacher
Copy the Battlefield Food Project Page (39) for each group. Use decaffeinated tea, hot cocoa, or dark juice in place of coffee.

Battlefield Food Project Page

North

Salt Horse

A slang term for salted beef issued by the Northern army. So salty it lasted two years before decaying. Soldiers soaked it for hours before they could stand to eat it.

Ingredients
- packaged beef jerky
- water

Directions
1. Break beef jerky into small pieces.
2. Soak jerky in a bowl of water until softened.

Bully Soup

Northern hot cereal consisting of cornmeal, crushed hardtack, wine, ginger, and water, all cooked together.

Ingredients
- 1 cup (240 ml) cornmeal
- 5 cups (1.18 L) water
- saltine crackers, crumbled
- ground ginger to taste

Directions
1. Combine cornmeal and 1 cup (240 ml) water in a saucepan.
2. Add remaining ingredients and cook, stirring constantly, until thickened.

South

Cush

Confederate stew made with bacon, cornbread, and water, cooked until the water evaporated.

Ingredients
- bacon, cooked and broken into small pieces
- cornbread
- water

Directions
1. Break cornbread into small pieces.
2. Combine bacon and cornbread with enough water to soak cornbread.

Artificial Oysters

Southern mixture of grated green corn mixed with egg and butter, then rolled and fried.

Ingredients
- 1 cup (240 ml) cream-style corn
- 2 eggs, beaten
- 6 Tbsp. (90 ml) flour
- ½ tsp. (2.5 ml) baking powder
- butter for frying

Directions
1. Combine ingredients in bowl.
2. Drop by spoonfuls into butter in frying pan. Cook on one side until brown. Turn over and brown other side.

Jefferson Davis

Jefferson Davis, as president of the Confederate States of America, came to be the symbol for the convictions of the South. Davis was an experienced statesman, serving as a Democrat in the U.S. House of Representatives and the U.S. Senate. He made many improvements for the armed forces as secretary of war under President Franklin Pierce. Davis had a distinguished military career, serving in the Black Hawk Wars. He was a serious student of the Constitution and political philosophy.

Davis was elected to the provisional presidency of the Confederacy in February, 1861, and to the presidency in 1862. Davis wanted to finance the war by imposing taxes, but the Confederate states opposed him on this issue. So they borrowed and printed large amounts of paper currency, which eventually led to high inflation. He was not a popular leader, and many Southerners criticized his running of the war. However, he gained the respect of many during his imprisonment after the war, and his lifelong defense of the Southern cause made him a symbol of the South's ideals.

Project
Research and write a report on Jefferson Davis and the Confederacy.

Materials
- Confederate Flag page
- research materials

Directions
1. Research the Confederate States of America. What did they believe in and stand for? Why were they fighting the Civil War?
2. Research Jefferson Davis. What made him a good president for the Confederacy? Where was he from and what did he believe regarding the Confederate goals?
3. Use the information you learn to write a report about the Confederate States and their president, Jefferson Davis.
4. Color the Confederate Flag, and include it as the cover of your report.

For the Teacher
Make one copy of the Confederate Flag (page 42) per student.

Abraham Lincoln

Abraham Lincoln's primary goal during the Civil War was to keep the nation united. Born on the American frontier and largely self-educated, he had a tremendous belief that whether slavery was abolished or not, one strong nation was far better than two weaker nations. As a young man, Lincoln served briefly in the military during the Black Hawk War. He worked at several careers: storekeeper, postmaster, surveyor, and finally lawyer. He served four terms in the Illinois legislature, and one term in the U.S. House of Representatives as a Whig. In 1856, he joined the two-year-old antislavery Republican party, and became an influential speaker on the party's behalf. As presidential nominee in 1860, Lincoln won the presidency with less than 40 percent of the popular vote.

Lincoln's election was the trigger that caused the first of the Southern states to secede from the Union, precipitating the start of the Civil War. Many of Lincoln's war-time policies were unpopular. He was the chief architect of the Union's military strategy and he was often in conflict with his own military leaders. Lincoln took a personal interest in the people involved in the war, and took time to see widows and children of his soldiers. By the time of his second election in 1864, the war had taken a dreadful toll on his health and strength. On April 14, 1865, five days after Lee's surrender to Grant, Lincoln was assassinated.

Project
Research and write a report on Abraham Lincoln and the Union.

Materials
- Union Flag page
- research materials

Directions
1. Research the Union during the Civil War era. What did they believe in and stand for? Why were they fighting the Civil War?
2. Research Abraham Lincoln. What made him a good president for the Union? Where was he from and what did he believe regarding the Union's goals?
3. Use the information you learn to write a report about the Union and their president, Abraham Lincoln.
4. Color the Union Flag, and include it as the cover of your report.

For the Teacher
Make one copy of the Union Flag (page 43) per student.

Confederate Flag

42 People

EP108 Civil War © Highsmith® Inc. 2007

Union Flag

Ulysses S. Grant

Ulysses S. Grant was an unusual person. Except for soldiering, he failed at most everything else he tried to do. In the years between the Mexican War (where he served with distinction) and the Civil War, he unsuccessfully tried his hand at a number of occupations. Even his two terms as president after the Civil War were marked by failure and corruption.

But Ulysses S. Grant could lead an army. When the Civil War broke out in 1861, he enlisted in the Union Army and was made a colonel. He rose quickly through the ranks. President Lincoln took notice of his ability and promoted him to the rank of brigadier general. One victory after another followed on the battlefield, and in 1864, Lincoln made him head of all Union forces.

Ulysses Grant's battlefield strategy was simple: hammer away at the enemy with everything you have until you wear him down. Such tactics led to the surrender of the Confederacy on April 9, 1865.

Project

Make a mondala. A mondala is a circle that is divided into four sections. Each section contains a picture that tells something about the person it pertains to.

Materials

- white paper
- pencil or pen
- crayons or colored pencils

Directions

1. Draw a circle about 6 inches in diameter on the top portion of a piece of white paper. Using a ruler, divide the circle into four equal parts.
2. In the upper left-hand quarter of the circle, attach the picture of Ulysses S. Grant.
3. In the second, third, and fourth quarters of your mondala, draw pictures having to do with Ulysses S. Grant's career. Consult other sources for additional information.
4. At the bottom of your mondala, briefly explain what each of your pictures stands for.

For the Teacher

Copy one picture of Ulysses S. Grant (right) per student.

Robert E. Lee

Robert E. Lee was one of the prominent generals of the Confederacy, but he was admired greatly by both the North and the South. His father was a famous cavalry leader in the Revolutionary War. Lee graduated with honors from West Point and had a distinguished military career.

When his home state of Virginia seceded from the Union, Lee faced a dilemma. He did not believe in secession, but could not fight against family and friends. He took charge of the Army of Virginia, even though Lincoln had asked him to head the Union army. When he was forced to surrender to General Grant on April 9, 1865, Lee represented the Southern troops with honor, in full dress uniform, complete with sword.

Project
Write letters to Lincoln or Davis accepting the position of general.

Materials
- notebook paper

Directions
1. Imagine that you are in the United States army during the Civil War, and you have been asked to join both sides as a general. Brainstorm the pros and cons of joining each side.
2. Decide which offer you would accept. Write a letter to either Jefferson Davis or Abraham Lincoln in which you accept the position, explaining your reasons for your decision.
3. After writing your letter, participate in a class discussion about the decision that Robert E. Lee had to make.

For the Teacher
During the class discussion, ask students to think about how Robert E. Lee made the decision to join the Confederate army. If you like, create an imaginary situation where they would have to make a similar choice.

General Sherman

William Tecumseh Sherman was one of the most prominent generals of the Union army. He commanded forces at the battles of Bull Run and Shiloh and took part in the capture of Vicksburg. In 1864, he came under the command of Ulysses S. Grant, who appointed Sherman the commander of Union forces in the West.

With three armies totaling 100,000 men, he captured Atlanta, and then began his famous "March to the Sea." His entire army marched across Georgia, destroying the last of the South's economic resources. With Georgia conquered, Sherman then moved through South Carolina.

Project
Research Sherman's march across Georgia and South Carolina. Create a map outlining the route.

Materials
- reference books
- U.S. map
- butcher paper
- pencils
- markers

Directions
1. Use reference books to create a written outline of Sherman's route.
2. Use a U.S. map to recreate a map of the area covered, including details like mountains, bodies of water, and cities.
3. Trace Sherman's path, marking the progress with available dates.

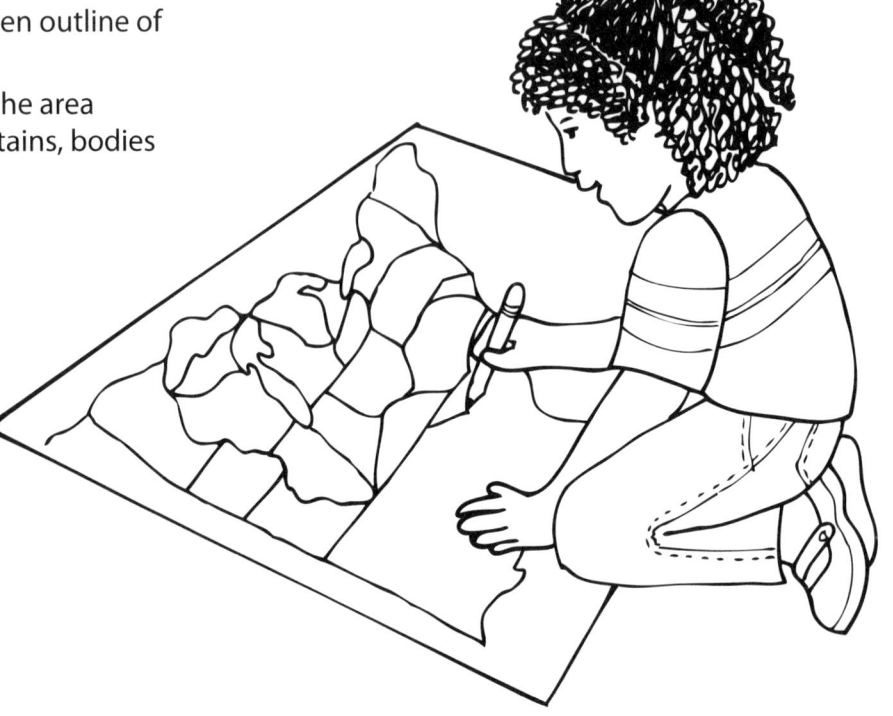

Literature List

This is just a sampling of the many fine books, both fiction and nonfiction, written about the Civil War. *Rifles for Watie* by Harold Keith won the Newbery Medal in 1959, *The Perilous Road* by William O. Steele and *Across Five Aprils* by Irene Hunt were Newbery Honor Books in 1958 and 1965 respectively, and *Abraham Lincoln: A Photobiography* was awarded the Newbery Medal in 1987. Check with your librarian for further recommendations.

Bull Run
by Paul Fleischman. HarperCollins, 1993. 112 p. Gr. 4–8
Northerners, Southerners, generals, couriers, dreaming boys, and worried sisters describe the glory, the horror, the thrill, and the disillusionment of the first battle of the Civil War.

Civil War A to Z
by Norman Bolotin. Dutton Children's Books, 2002. 148 p. Gr. 4–8
Alphabetically arranged articles present more than 100 people, places, and points of importance of the Civil War.

Duel of the Ironclads: The Monitor vs. the Virginia
by Patrick O'Brien. Walker, 2003. 40 p. Gr. 3–6
A description of the construction, battles, and historical impact of the Civil War battleships the *Monitor* and the *Virginia*, known to Union forces as the *Monitor* and the *Merrimack*, which focuses on the Battle of Hampton Roads.

Hold the Flag High
by Catherine Clinton. Katherine Tegen Books, 2005. 32 p. Gr. 2–5
Describes the Civil War battle of Morris Island, South Carolina, during which Sergeant William H. Carney became the first African American to earn a Congressional Medal of Honor by preserving the flag.

Jefferson Davis (American War Biographies)
by E. J. Carter. Heinemann, 2004. 48 p. Gr. 3–6
Profiles Jefferson Davis, who proved himself as a soldier in the Mexican War but had mixed success and failure as president of the Confederate States of America during the Civil War.

Li'l Dan, the Drummer Boy: A Civil War Story
by Romare Bearden. Simon & Schuster, 2003. Book and CD edition. 40 p. Gr. 1–4
When a company of black Union soldiers tells Li'l Dan that he is no longer a slave, he follows them, and uses his beloved drum to save them from attack.

Photo by Brady: A Picture of the Civil War
by Jennifer Armstrong. Atheneum, 2005. 147 p. Gr. 5–8
The story of the Civil War as seen through the lenses of the field photographers hired by Matthew Brady, who traveled with troops and made visual records of what they saw.

Pink and Say
by Patricia Polacco. Philomel, 1994. 32 p. Gr. 3–6
Say Curtis describes his meeting with Pinkus Aylee, a black soldier, during the Civil War, and their capture by Southern troops. Based on a true story about the author's great-great-grandfather.

Robert E. Lee: Confederate Commander
by Jennifer Blizin Gillis. Compass Point Books, 2005. 112 p. Gr. 5–7
Biography of the confederate general.

United No More! Stories of the Civil War
by Doreen Rappaport and Joan Verniero. HarperCollins, 2005. 132 p. Gr. 4–7
Seven stories of real people whose important acts made them a part of history.

Glossary

abolitionist—a person who worked to end slavery in the United States

artillery—a branch of the armed forces that operates large mounted guns, too heavy to carry; also, the guns themselves

bayonet—a long, narrow-bladed knife designed to fit on the end of a rifle barrel and to be used in hand-to-hand combat

blockade—means used to prevent the entry and exit of ships from a harbor

carte de visite—card printed with miniature portraits and used as calling cards

casualty—a soldier who is killed, wounded, captured, or missing in action during battle

cavalry—a branch of the army trained to fight on horseback

Confederate States of America—the alliance of 11 southern states that withdrew from the United States in 1860 and 1861: Alabama, Arkansas, Florida, Georgia, Louisiana, Mississippi, North Carolina, South Carolina, Tennessee, Texas, and Virginia; also referred to as the Confederacy

contraband—any good that has been illegally traded or smuggled; during the Civil War this was especially a slave who escaped to or was brought behind Union lines

Democrat—a member of the political party that supported slavery and believed states should control their own affairs without interference from the national government

draft—the government's selection of citizens for a required period of military service

emancipate—to free from slavery

Emancipation Proclamation—an act issued by President Lincoln in 1862 that freed all slaves in the rebel states

enlist—to join the armed services

Federal—having to do with the union of states that recognized the authority of the United States government based in Washington, D.C.

hardtack—hard flour and water biscuits

haversack—a canvas bag used for carrying personal items

housewife—small sewing kit carried by soldiers

infantry—a branch of the army made up of units trained to fight on foot

kepi—military cap with a circular, flattened top and visor

rations—daily food allowances

Rebel—another term for a Confederate soldier or a civilian supporter of the Confederacy

sutlers—peddlers who followed troops from camp to camp

Union—another name for the United States of America, used especially during the Civil War

Yankee—another name for a Northerner